CONTE

DEDICATION

This book is dedicated to Dr. Gary Chapman,

author of The Five Love Languages.

Gary,

I'll always be grateful to God for using you to introduce me to Christ. Thanks for taking the time to invest your life in mine. In doing so, you taught me discipleship. Few earthly events are more fulfilling and incredibly exciting as to invest your life into someone else's, watching them grow in their faith in Christ. This is experiencing discipleship. I now understand that you haven't made a disciple until your disciple has made a disciple.

Clarence Shuler

2 Timothy 2:2

Experiencing DISCIPLESHIP

A Small Group Faith-Building Adventure

Clarence Shuler

Loveland, Colorado

R.E.A.L. Guarantee to you:

This Group resource incorporates our R.E.A.L. approach to ministry—one that encourages long-term retention and life transformation. It's ministry that's:

Relational
Because learner-to-learner interaction enhances learning and builds Christian friendships.

Experiential
Because what learners experience through discussion and action sticks with them up to 9 times longer than what they simply hear or read.

Applicable
Because the aim of Christian education is to equip learners to be both hearers and doers of God's Word.

Learner-based
Because learners understand and retain more when the learning process takes into consideration how they learn best.

Credits
Editors: Mikal Keefer and Matt Lockhart
Creative Development Editor: Dave Thornton
Chief Creative Officer: Joani Schultz
Copy Editor: Janis Sampson
Art Director: Kari K. Monson
Computer Graphic Artist: Stephen Beer
Cover Art Director/Designer: Jeff A. Storm
Cover Photography: Getty Images
Production Manager: Peggy Naylor

ISBN 0-7644-2406-8
10 9 8 7 6 5 4 3 2 1   11 10 09 08 07 06 05 04 03 02
Printed in the United States of America.

SESSION OVERVIEW

*T*he sessions in this study are designed to engage participants on multiple levels: relationally, through engaging small group interaction; mentally, through individual study in preparation for the group session; and spiritually, with a practical life application challenge as a part of each session. To facilitate these processes, each session is made up of the following components:

Loosening Up (15-20 minutes)

Initially, participants are given a chance to transition into the topic of study through engaging questions and activities, designed to start the session off on the right foot. This section also provides the opportunity for follow-up accountability for the previous session's Faith-Building Adventure.

Foundation (50-60 minutes)

Group Bible study provides a foundational platform for the entire session. Through a series of thoughtful, engaging, and relational questions, group members will open up their Bibles and hearts to study and discuss what God's Word has to say on the discipleship topic that is being examined.

Taking It to Heart (15-20 minutes)

This part of each session guides the group into a closing time that includes a review of Key Verses and a closing prayer time. Participants will also look ahead to what is coming up next.

Taking It to the House

Within this section participants will be challenged to apply personally the biblical principles they have studied. This will be done in two ways: (1) Each session includes a Faith-Building Adventure. These adventures provide group members with practical ways to experience discipleship. (2) The other feature in this section is Personal Preparation for the Next Session. Broken down into five daily ten-to-fifteen-minute segments to be completed between sessions, the Personal Preparation section provides group members the opportunity to delve into the Bible on their own. They can go deeper into Scripture, learning Key Verses and principles related to the next session's discipleship topic.

A WORD TO THE LEADER

Thanks for committing to lead an *Experiencing Discipleship* group. Making a disciple involves not only imparting biblical information, but also building a relationship with the disciple, or learner. So whether you have led a group before or not, here are a few suggestions to help you facilitate this course.

A Few General Notes

This course is designed primarily for use as a small group study. However, it's flexible enough in format to be used in a class setting as well. The small group setting is generally better in that enough time can be allowed per meeting to work through a complete session. And meeting somewhere other than church can sometimes make it easier to create a climate of community. If used in a class setting with a limited time frame, you will need to consider whether to focus only on the Foundation portion of the session (50-60 minutes) or to cover a session over more than one meeting time.

Set the tone from the beginning that your group is a safe place, a place of acceptance. And although this course is oriented toward Christians, be sensitive that you may have people in your group who are searching for God. Through this course, Christians and non-Christians alike can find answers to spiritual questions. Also be open to the idea of rotating sessions to different homes, if this is of interest to the group. Providing group members the opportunity to host a meeting is another way to build community.

An important part of this course is what group members do in between the group sessions. Strongly encourage group members to commit to completing each session's Taking It to the House components—the Faith-Building Adventure and the Personal Prep for the next session. The group sessions have been created in such a way that a person can participate and benefit from a session without necessarily having completed the "through the week" assignments. However, the discipleship experience of the course participants will be greatly enriched if they commit themselves to the personal application components. Be sure to lead by example by doing the application parts yourself. You'll be glad you did! As important as the personal application parts of each session are, group members should be encouraged to attend every session whether they have completed the Faith-Building Adventure and Personal Prep or not.

If you have led a group before, you know that a key dynamic is group interaction. To assist in getting everyone involved, the group questions and activities are designed to be interactive and relational. And throughout this course, you will find suggested use of subgroups for various questions and activities. If you have a "large" small group (more than eight people), consider having subgroups of four to seven people work through the Foundation questions. This will help keep the group on schedule and give everyone a chance to participate in the discussion. A co-leader, an apprentice leader, or, if married, your spouse might all be good candidates to help facilitate a subgroup.

A Few Specific Notes

Session One: The main goal of the first session is to get acquainted. Set a friendly tone by warmly greeting group members as they arrive. Introduce people to one another. And be sure to greet latecomers without making them feel guilty. You may want to serve refreshments first. That way, if people are a few minutes late they won't miss the beginning of the lesson material. Be "prayed up" and enlist prayer support for each of your sessions. You're on the front lines!

Please note: The *Session One* Faith-Building Adventure involves group members writing their faith stories. This is an important exercise for everyone to complete, as it becomes the basis for the Loosening Up opener in *Session Two*.

Session Two: Be prepared to receive copies of the group members' personal faith stories. Be faithful to read the ones you receive, and provide feedback in a timely manner to the individuals. (You may want to write notes on the copies of the faith stories and return them at the end of the next session, or send cards or e-mails with constructive comments.) For the opening activity, encourage all to share their faith stories. But don't force this. If someone wants to just listen, that's OK. Consider sharing your faith story last, to the whole group.

Session Seven: In the margin on page 110, you'll see a note that directs you to create a drawing to use for the Loosening Up activity. You'll want to do this in advance of this session. Base your drawing on the sample illustration on page 159.

Session Nine: The first part of question 4 (p. 143) asks about the steps Jesus took in reaching out to the woman at the well (this is also asked as a part of the prep for Session Nine—see Day 3, pages 135-136). While answers may vary, the steps that I have identified are as follows:

1. Jesus breaks the traditional law of the Jews by traveling in Samaria.

2. Jesus goes to where the Samaritan woman lives.

3. Jesus meets her on her own turf (at the well).

4. Jesus breaks another traditional law by speaking to a Samaritan woman.

5. Jesus makes himself vulnerable to the woman by asking for help.

6. Jesus has staying power. He doesn't leave when initially rejected.

May God richly bless you!

INTRODUCTION

*I*n trying to determine a name for this discipleship study, I found myself torn between the actual title, *Experiencing Discipleship*, and the runner-up, *The Discipleship Challenge*. God wants us to obey Christ's disciple-making command found in Matthew 28:19, "Therefore go and make disciples…" But I also believe God wants us to *experience* discipleship. And as we experience discipleship, we will find it *challenging*. Make no mistake about it—discipleship is work! There are materials to study, verses to learn, and schedules to adjust for the time it requires.

The primary purpose of *Experiencing Discipleship* isn't to give you more spiritual activity nor more biblical knowledge, even though these are byproducts. And to be certain, discipleship is a *faith-building* experience. However, it's not just gathering information but also requires building relationships. Biblical discipleship isn't an informational *or* a relational proposition; it's a *both-and* proposition. Through this course, you may build lifelong relationships with members of the group who are joining you on this adventure as a community where you can share your heart, your fears, and your dreams. Of course, this is dependent on the extent to which you become vulnerable to each other as you share your personal stories.

Experiencing Discipleship is also a *faith-building* experience because the Bible tells us in 2 Timothy 2:2, "And the things you have heard me say…entrust to reliable men [and women] who will also be qualified to teach others." This is the essence of discipleship: teaching others what you have learned and are learning about Christ. The goal of this study is to teach or reacquaint Christians with some basic biblical principles which can easily be taught to others. One of the faith-building aspects of this course is asking God to send you someone with whom you can share what you are learning and then by faith begin to invest your life in him or her.

The return on your spiritual investment is encouraging and gently challenging those you teach, to teach others (2 Timothy 2:2). You should always look for spiritual returns on your investments because God does (Matthew 25:14-30). Remember, you have not made a disciple until your disciple makes a disciple!

Yet the biggest personal challenge may be facing the vulnerable realization that the Holy Spirit desires to change our lives to be even more Christlike than we already are. It is this realization accompanied by vulnerability that opens the door for more intimacy with Christ. There is something about being challenged as disciples that helps us see and understand more clearly God's big picture. Maybe it's because we are obeying God by serving others. To me it's similar to being a parent. You begin to not only see but to also understand the cycle of physical life. This understanding often motivates us to change our priorities to what is really important and to what will last. This is the ultimate experience of making disciples. God wants us to experience personal fulfillment and purpose to the degree that can only be experienced through discipleship. So *Experiencing Discipleship* is about equipping you and about helping others. As you begin this study, think not only about your own spiritual growth but also about how God wants to use you to share what you learn with other brothers and sisters you have in Christ. I hope that this will also be a motivating force for you to complete all of your assignments in order to maximize your discipleship experience and better prepare you to teach others. My prayer is that at the end of this course you won't be the same! I hope you will find the challenge of discipleship a priceless experience!

Since the early 1970s, I have been involved with discipleship in one way or another because Dr. Gary Chapman began discipling me back in 1970. What a faith-building, life-changing experience it has been and continues to be for me. May you experience nothing less!

Your brother and servant in Christ,

Clarence Shuler
President/CEO, Building Lasting Relationships, Inc.
www.blrcentral.org
Hebrews 13:20-21

Session ONE

Getting Acquainted

Leader: In preparing to lead this course, if you haven't done so already, please read the "Session Overview" (starting on page 5) and "A Word to the Leader" (starting on page 7).

Discipleship Objective 1:

To begin the process of becoming a Christian community—a safe place to discuss spiritual things and to receive support and encouragement as you experience discipleship.

Loosening Up (15-20 minutes)

Getting to Know You

Introduce yourself to the group, and then help others get to know you by telling the group:

- your occupation,

- a favorite hobby or interest you have (or what you would like to do *if* you had the time), and

- how long you have been a Christian (if you're unsure if you are a Christian, share what you would like to gain from this study or where you see yourself in your spiritual journey).

Group Directory

Pass your books around the room with everyone writing his or her name, phone number, and e-mail address in the space provided.

Name, Phone, and E-Mail

Name, Phone, and E-Mail

Name, Phone, and E-Mail

Name, Phone, and E-Mail

_____

Name, Phone, and E-Mail

_____

Name, Phone, and E-Mail

_____

Name, Phone, and E-Mail

_____

Name, Phone, and E-Mail

Foundation (50-60 minutes)

GREAT EXPECTATIONS

1. What sparked your interest about this discipleship course?

2. What do you hope to gain from participating in this group and study?

> If you have a large group, form smaller groups (of around four to seven people) to answer the group discussion questions. Unless otherwise noted, answer the questions in your subgroup. At the end of the Foundation section, allow time for subgroups to report their answers to the whole group.

A STORY OF FAITH

In the book of Acts, the Apostle Paul tells about his journey to faith in Christ. Form two groups, with each group taking one of the following Scripture passages:

- Acts 22:1-22

- Acts 26:1-23

In your group, read your passage and then discuss questions 3-6.

3. How would you summarize in a brief outline the events that took place in the passage you read?

4. What was Paul's life like before his personal encounter with Jesus?

5. How would you describe what happened to Paul?

6. What was different about Paul after his encounter with Jesus?

After each group has had time to answer these questions, have a spokesperson from each group give a report to the whole group.

7. How are these two accounts similar? different?

Before discussing the following questions (8-10), take a few minutes to reflect on these questions. You may want to jot down your answers.

Your Faith Story

8. Before encountering Christ, what was your life like?

9. How did God "get your attention"? How did you respond?

10. How has your life changed since you entered into a personal relationship with Christ?

Taking It to Heart (15-20 minutes)

TALKING TO GOD

Before closing this session in prayer, take a few minutes to share prayer requests. You may want to record prayer requests from the group in the space that follows.

Prayer Requests:

Looking Ahead: The discipleship focus in Session Two is examining what it means to be a Christian. To get the most out of this *Experiencing Discipleship* course, you are strongly encouraged to complete the Taking It to the House section before the next session.

Included within the Taking It to the House section are two parts:

1. *Faith-Building Adventure*

This is your opportunity to grow in your faith by making a personal application from the session you just studied.

2. *Personal Prep for the Next Session*

This is an in-depth study related to the content you will be discussing at your next group meeting. You are encouraged to study this material through the week prior to the next meeting. To do this will require discipline. Plan to make it a part of your schedule—it will be worth it!

Taking It to the House

FAITH-BUILDING ADVENTURE

Welcome to the first Faith-Building Adventure of *Experiencing Discipleship*. Your adventure for this week is to write your faith story. Your personal faith story is one of the most effective and powerful tools you have to tell others about Jesus.

To assist you in this process of creating your faith story, following is a faith story outline and a sample faith story.

Faith Story Outline

I. A faith story is the telling of how you came to a personal relationship with Jesus. It's told for the purpose of establishing the fact and credibility of your new life in Christ.

II. Some Basic Characteristics of a Personal Faith Story

    A. Your faith story has authority. It's your own personal experience.

    B. Your faith story communicates and relates because it's vital, fresh, and alive!

III. Outline of a Personal Faith Story

    A. Your life before you met Jesus

    B. Your realization of your need for Christ

    C. Your faith commitment experience

    D. Your life after making a personal commitment to Christ

IV. Critical Criteria in Preparing Your Personal Faith Story

    A. Keep your faith story short and simple (three to five minutes)!

    B. Keep your faith story to the point.

    C. Give adequate details.

    D. Keep it positive (avoid bragging and negative statements, and be careful about using names of people in a negative manner).

    E. Use language non-Christians and people who don't attend church can understand.

    F. Keep refining and rewriting your faith story.

SAMPLE FAITH STORY

Clarence Shuler's Faith Story

I met Jesus Christ on May 8, 1970, at a retreat in Hillsville, Virginia. I knew a little about Jesus because I was forced to go to

Sunday school and church until I was fourteen. Naturally, as soon as I had a say in this matter, I stopped going to church.

It was also at the age of fourteen that I met a guy named Russell Harper, who was my best friend for the next four years. Basketball was my god and I was a devoted worshipper. I was born and bred in North Carolina, where we have basketball, tobacco, and Baptists—pretty much in that order.

Russell went to an integrated school and I went to an all-black school. Some of Russell's white friends invited him to their church. Their church had just built a gym. Russell didn't want to be the only black in the gym, so he asked me to go with him. I didn't care who was going to be there if we were going to play basketball!

The people were very nice. I was shocked because these were white people in North Carolina in 1968 and racial tension was high.

We played basketball for a while, and then everyone sat down. We had a discussion on Christians and dating. It was pretty good. The next week, it was about the Christian and sex. Each week it was something relevant. The discussion would usually last one hour, then you could play basketball for another hour. Dr. Gary Chapman, who led the discussions, would then tell us each week how we could accept Jesus Christ into our hearts as our personal Savior and Lord.

I kept going for the next two years. I don't remember missing a single Saturday night. I was popular at school, my family was well-off financially (or at least I thought we were), and I had a nice girlfriend. However, I began to see that the people in this church had something in their lives that I was missing. For two years, I watched Gary's lifestyle. He was the most Christlike person that I had ever met. He still is!

There were a lot of things with which I was struggling, such as my lack of height, racial prejudice, insecurity, and my parents, who always seemed to be on my case.

On a youth retreat in Virginia in May of 1970, Gary preached a sermon which basically asked this question: Is your life complete, or is something missing? I realized something was missing in my life. I had thought that if I made the high school basketball team, all of my needs would be met. They were not! The glory of basketball would always fade away. I needed Jesus Christ in my life.

On May 8, I asked Jesus Christ to forgive me for my sins and to come into my life as my Lord and Savior and to make my life what he wanted it to be. Gary had shared John 3:16 with me: "God so loved [Clarence] that he gave his one and only Son, that whoever believes in him shall not perish but have eternal life."

My life changed dramatically! God gave me an inner peace that stays with me no matter what the situation. God also taught me to accept myself the way I am. I learned the freedom of being an individual, which began transforming me into a leader. Most of all, I began to live the wonderful life God had already planned for me before I was even born (Psalm 139:14-16).

Now it's your turn! Write your faith story following the outline (pp. 18-19). Remember, keep it short and simple. If you can, keep it to no more than two pages in length.

Your Faith Story

Write your faith story in the space provided. If you use a separate piece of paper to write your faith story, be sure to bring it with you to the next group meeting. If you write your faith story in this book, and you would like to have your group leader review your story to provide feedback to you, be sure to make a copy for your leader and bring it to the next session.

PERSONAL PREP FOR SESSION TWO

The discipleship focus in Session Two is on having a solid biblical understanding of what a Christian is. You are encouraged to spend ten to fifteen minutes a day over the course of five days in preparation for the next session.

Key Verses for Session Two

- John 5:24

- Romans 6:23

- Romans 10:9-10

As you spend time in preparation for Session Two, work on learning these Key Verses. Try and commit to memory at least one (your choice) of these passages. At the end of Session Two in a small group of two or three, you will be given the opportunity to review the verse or verses you learned.

The Baggage From Our Past

Look up the following verses. For each verse write in your own words what that verse communicates to you.

- Isaiah 53:6

_____

_____

- Romans 3:10

_____

_____

- Romans 3:23

- Romans 5:12

According to these verses, what separates people from God?

God's Provision

Look up the following verses. For each verse, write in your own words what that verse communicates to you.

- Acts 4:12

- Romans 5:8

- Romans 6:23

• Romans 10:9-10

_____

_____

• Ephesians 2:8-9

_____

_____

According to these verses, what remedy has God provided to us for our sin condition?

_____

_____

DAY 3

Discerning Christians

We can see from Scripture that Jesus can remove the baggage of our past. Such life-changing facts may lead us to another question: Is it possible to discern whether or not someone else is a Christian?

Because of the ministry of the Holy Spirit in a Christian's life, it's possible for Christians to recognize another Christian. However, caution is critical when trying to determine if someone is a Christian. Unfortunately, some people and groups are extremely legalistic and judgmental about this issue. Yet there are certain characteristics that generally serve as good indicators that a person is a Christian.

Read Romans 8:14-16. According to these verses, what are some indicators a person is a Christian?

_____

_____

Characteristics of a Relationship With Christ

The following characteristics from Scripture can help us to discern if someone is a Christian. Again, look up the following Scriptures and write in your own words what they say to you.

• Romans 15:13

_____

_____

• 2 Corinthians 5:17

_____

_____

• Galatians 2:20

_____

_____

• Galatians 5:22-23

_____

_____

• 1 John 3:9-10

_____

_____

How would you summarize what these verses say are key indicators of a relationship with Christ?

_____

_____

DAY 4

Being Sure of Your Faith

Just as there are basic characteristics that Christians should demonstrate in their lives as they grow and mature in their faith, there are basic indicators we should recognize in ourselves to confirm that we are Christians.

When people are insecure or not sure about something, they tend not to develop in that area due to a lack of confidence. Likewise, when people are insecure or unsure about their faith, they tend not to develop or grow due to a lack of confidence. Being able to grow as a Christian is often dependent on the Christian being confident in his or her relationship with Christ.

Having confidence that you have Jesus Christ in your life is the springboard for both your personal growth in Christ and your ability to help others in the body of Christ grow toward maturity.

If you are not sure if you are a Christian, the following verses should help to provide clarity for you. (You know the drill: Write the meaning of the following verses in your own words.)

- Romans 10:9-13

- 1 John 2:3-6

- 1 John 3:14

- 1 John 3:23-24

_____

_____

- 1 John 4:13-16

_____

_____

- 1 John 5:1-5

_____

_____

Based on the content of the preceding verses, finish this statement:

"I can have assurance that I have a relationship with Jesus Christ because _____."

If you are unsure about whether you have a personal relationship with Christ, I encourage you to pray, reflecting on the verses you have studied. Recognize that you are separated from God by sin, and "confess with your mouth, 'Jesus is Lord,' and believe in your heart that God raised him from the dead" (Romans 10:9). Also talk to your group leader or pastor about how you are feeling and any questions you have.

DAY 5

Having Confidence as a Christian

Look up the following verses. For each verse, write in your own words what that verse communicates to you.

- Matthew 28:20b

_____

_____

• John 10:27-29

_____

_____

• 2 Corinthians 5:5

_____

_____

• Ephesians 1:13-14

_____

_____

How do you feel after reading these verses? Why?

_____

_____

What questions do you have that came out of this study in preparation for Session Two?

_____

_____

_____

_____

Session TWO

The Measure of a Christian

DISCIPLESHIP OBJECTIVE 2:

To be able to experience Christian discipleship, it's important for you to be confident in your faith and have a solid biblical understanding of what a Christian is.

Loosening Up (15-20 minutes)

FAITH-BUILDING FOLLOW-UP

> If you completed last session's Faith-Building Adventure of writing your faith story and you made a copy for the leader, give it to him or her now.

Begin this session by sharing your faith story with two other people. In groups of three, take turns sharing your faith story. After all the groups are finished, discuss this question:

• What is one thing you enjoyed about hearing someone else's faith story?

Foundation (50-60 minutes)

WHAT MAKES SOMEONE A CHRISTIAN?

> If you have a large group, form smaller groups to answer the group discussion questions. Unless otherwise noted, answer the questions in your subgroup. At the end of the Foundation section, allow time for subgroups to report their answers to the whole group.

1. What are some common misperceptions that people have about what makes someone a Christian?

2. What do you think makes someone a Christian?

3. How do your answers to question 2 contrast with the responses you discussed in question 1?

4. In groups of two or three, select one or two of the following Scriptures. In your group, read your verse(s) and discuss what your Bible passage says about being a Christian.

- Acts 4:12
- Romans 5:12
- Romans 3:10
- Romans 6:23
- Romans 3:23
- Romans 10:9-10
- Romans 5:8
- Ephesians 2:8-9

After a few minutes, report to the whole group. Read your verses and share your insights. As a group, discuss how these verses relate to each other.

5. What is the difference between having religion and being a Christian?

CHARACTERISTICS OF A CHRISTIAN

6. How would you respond if a non-Christian asked you how can you tell if someone is a Christian?

7. In groups of two or three, select two or three of the following Scriptures. In your group read your verses and discuss how your passages relate to the question: How can you tell if someone is a Christian?

- Romans 8:14-16
- Romans 10:9-13
- 2 Corinthians 5:17
- Galatians 2:20

- Galatians 5:22-23
- 1 John 2:3-6
- 1 John 3:23-24
- 1 John 4:13-16

After a few minutes, each group should take turns sharing their verses and insights with the whole group.

8. From looking at the verses in the previous questions (4 and 7), what did you find to be the most comforting, convicting, or challenging?

9. Is it possible or reasonable to expect that a Christian will exhibit these characteristics at all times? Explain. (If you can, back up your position from Scripture.)

BEING CONFIDENT AS A CHRISTIAN

10. Read the following verses:

- Matthew 28:20b
- John 10:27-29

- 2 Corinthians 5:5

- Ephesians 1:13-14

From these verses, what hope can Christians have in their relationship with Christ?

Taking It to Heart (15-20 minutes)

KEY VERSES

Form groups of two or three and review the Key Verses for this session:

- John 5:24

- Romans 6:23

- Romans 10:9-10

TALKING TO GOD

Before closing in prayer, share prayer requests. Be sure to include any updates to requests that were shared in the previous session.

Prayer Requests:

Looking Ahead: The discipleship focus in Session Three is on the importance of serving Jesus as Lord. As a reminder, between now and the next session, you should try and complete this session's Faith-Building Adventure as well as invest time in individual study to prepare for the next session.

Taking It to the House

FAITH-BUILDING ADVENTURE

Between now and the next session, plan to share your personal faith story with at least one person. Try to share it with a non-Christian friend, by asking them to critique it. Tell your friend it's an assignment from the Bible study you are in and you would appreciate his or her help. Ask for your friend's critique.

To help prepare you for this assignment, review the following tips about preparing to share your faith story.

Sharing Your Faith Story

1. Be prepared.

2. Practice: Share your faith story with a mature Christian friend, asking them for constructive criticism.

3. Practice some more: Share your faith story with non-Christians. Be creative in sharing your faith story with non-Christians. Have them listen to it and ask them to critique it. You can tell them you are doing it for a church-related class, which is true. This is one way to share your faith with your non-Christian friends without putting them on the defensive.

4. Incorporate it in your everyday conversation and lifestyle.

5. Use it in formal settings as speaking opportunities arise.

6. Remember to keep it short (five minutes or less)! Be sensitive not to abuse the time people give you to share about your faith. You don't want to turn someone off to the gospel, making it difficult for the next person that tells him or her about Jesus. People can always ask to hear more.

7. Ask God to bless you and others who hear your faith story.

PERSONAL PREP FOR SESSION THREE

The discipleship focus in Session Three is on serving Jesus as Lord. You are encouraged to spend approximately ten minutes a day over the next week preparing for the next group session.

DAY 1

Key Verses for Session Three

- Luke 6:46

- Luke 9:23-25

As you spend time in preparation for Session Three, work on learning these Key Verses. Try and commit to memory at least one (your choice) of the Scripture passages. As a part of the close in Session Three, you will have the opportunity to review your verse(s).

Jesus Christ Has the Right to Be Our Lord

Look up the Scripture references that follow, and complete the accompanying sentences.

- Read Romans 14:9.

"Jesus Christ is Lord because _____ ."

- Read Colossians 1:16-18.

"Jesus Christ is Lord because _____ ."

• Read 1 John 5:11-12.

"Jesus Christ is Lord because _____ ."

DAY 2

What Does "Jesus is Lord" Mean?

The word *lord* in the Greek (the primary language of the New Testament) has several different meanings. One definition, which has oriental roots, is *absolute sovereign*. Such a ruler is considered a god by his subjects. So when he or she speaks, that word is law. Seldom were these laws changed because gods don't make mistakes. For example, in the book of Daniel, Darius the Mede couldn't save Daniel from the lions' den, even though he wanted to (Daniel 5:31–6:28). Jesus Christ, however, is the perfect absolute sovereign—an all-knowing, all-seeing, all-powerful Lord.

Another definition for *lord* is owner or possessor. Also included in the definition is the idea of having all authority, love, and wisdom. An additional aspect of this word is the servant's (slave's) willingness to submit to his or her lord.

Master is another definition for lord. Jesus Christ is unlimited in power and the perfect master who *always* has his subjects' best interests as a priority.

It was not uncommon for some Old Testament Hebrew slave owners to treat their Hebrew slaves so well that the slaves didn't want to leave even when they were legally able to do so according to Hebrew law. Deuteronomy 15:16-17 tells the price that slaves had to pay if they were so devoted to their master that they wanted to remain slaves to their master.

From the moment the slave's ear was pierced, he or she (there were also women slaves) became a servant for life. The slave voluntarily relinquished freedom out of love for an earthly lord. Jesus Christ, the *perfect master,* provides the opportunity for us to yield to his Lordship because God has been and continues to be so good to us and for us!

[After becoming a Christian] I loved all mankind, slaveholders not excepted, though I abhorred slavery more than ever. I saw the world in a new light...I have gathered scattered pages of the Bible from the filthy street-gutters, and washed and dried them, that in moments of leisure I might get a word or two of wisdom from them.

— Ex-slave Fredrick Douglass

These words by Fredrick Douglass are words of a man who has yielded to the Lordship of Jesus Christ. We see in his words forgiveness of those who enslaved him and a passion for God's Word. A former slave has demonstrated some characteristics of a Christian who is yielding to the Lordship of Jesus Christ.

What Is Required for Me to Serve Jesus as Lord?

In Luke 9:23-25, Jesus gives the requirements necessary for his lordship to be put into action in the life of a Christian. Read Luke 9:23-25 and list as many things from this passage as you can that Jesus asks of a follower.

———————————————————————————————

———————————————————————————————

To deny oneself is to have Christ on the throne in our lives. This doesn't mean you aren't important. You still have interests. You are not a robot or a computer. It does mean that everything and everyone comes in second to Christ.

Often when "taking up one's cross" is mentioned, people are only told about their responsibilities as Christians. Taking up one's cross can also include experiencing all God has to offer Christians.

Luke 9:23-25 seems to imply that *following* Jesus may cost you everything you have, even your earthly life!

In Luke 9:22, Jesus foretold his suffering, rejection, death, and ultimate resurrection. Christians should be aware that living out the lordship of Christ—*denying yourself, taking up your cross, and following Christ*—may include all aspects of commitment to God that Christ demonstrated (for no servant is above his or her master—Matthew 10:24). Christians are to be obedient to these commands.

DAY 3

Characteristics of a Lordship Disciple

When we give God charge over our lives, we turn over the keys to our life. While yielding control can be a scary proposition, Jesus tells us to "Take my yoke upon you and learn from me…for my yoke is easy and my burden is light" (Matthew 11:29-30). And Christ doesn't ask us to do anything that he hasn't done.

In Philippians 2:6-8, Paul illustrates the character of Christ. Paul begins this incredible passage of Scripture by saying, "Your attitude should be the same as that of Christ Jesus," which is to say that since Christians have the Holy Spirit indwelling them, they can know what God's will for them is. As we obey God's will, we become *like* Christ. When a Christian has the mind of Christ, then he or she becomes like Jesus Christ.

According to Philippians 2:6-8, what attitude did Jesus Christ demonstrate?

These Philippians 2:6-8 characteristics belong to Jesus Christ. Since as Christians we belong to Christ, we can exhibit these same characteristics. As we continually make ourselves available to Jesus Christ as Lord, these characteristics will reproduce themselves in our lives.

Refer again to Philippians 2:6-8, and jot down the character traits of Jesus Christ in the chart that follows. Then write how these can be demonstrated in your life.

Christ's Character	My Character

Now read Philippians 2:9. What did God do for Jesus and why?

_____

_____

Read Philippians 2:10-11. What two things will every person have to do before Christ?

_____

_____

Just as a trophy "glorifies" the person who won it, so the life of the person who yields to Jesus as Lord, glorifies Jesus. This happens when every aspect of our being is made available to his purposes.

DAY 4

Roadblocks to Christ's Lordship

The more we understand the Lordship of Christ, the more we will understand that we (Christians) are Christ's servants (slaves).

Our decision to yield to Christ's Lordship may be met with some roadblocks or obstacles. The following is a list of possible roadblocks to experiencing Jesus as Lord.

Addiction	Money	Sex
Bitterness	Pleasure	Temper
Critical Spirit	Position	Things
Envy	Power	Thought-Life
Escapism	Pride	Tongue
Family	Priorities	Work
Fear	Recreation	Worry
Hobbies	Self-Effort	

From the list of roadblocks, which would you identify as problem areas for you? Circle these items.

What else can you think of that is an area that causes you to struggle as you attempt to yield to Christ?

_____

_____

Review the roadblocks you have identified, and list them on the chart that follows. Then record how you see each roadblock in your life, and think about what needs to happen to clear each roadblock.

Roadblocks to Christ's Lordship	How I See This in My Life	The Solution

Experiencing Christ's lordship is a decision. We do not make Christ Lord. He is Lord whether we treat him that way or not. The issue of whether we experience Christ as Lord in our daily lives depends on our willingness to yield to Christ. Jesus will not force his lordship upon us.

DAY 5

Experiencing Christ's Lordship in Your Life

This is the real deal! This is hopefully where our theology becomes reality. We must act *now* on what we know.

Desire—We must want Jesus Christ as our Lord.

Decision—We must decide by an act of the will for Jesus to be Lord of our life. There is no better time than right now!

Die to Self—We must die to self if we are to live for God. This doesn't require losing all interest in ourselves, but it does demand putting those desires in second place behind God's will, which must have first place in our lives.

If you desire to have Jesus as Lord of your life, here are some practical steps that can help you in this process:

1. *Confess your sins to God.* Read 1 John 1:9. Then write down your sins on a sheet of paper. Confess your sins to God and ask for forgiveness. Tear up your sheet of paper and throw it away. Then read Psalm 103:12.

2. *Ask God to control you by the Holy Spirit.*

3. *Seek to continually yield every area of your life to Christ.*

4. *Practice daily spiritual disciplines.* Spend "quiet time" with God (the subject of Session Four) and time in prayer (the subject of Session Five).

5. *Practice weekly spiritual disciplines:* Bible study (the subject of Session Six), learning Scripture, telling others about Jesus, and worshipping God in a Bible-believing church.

6. *Be spiritually accountable to someone.* Be in a relationship with a mature Christian who will encourage you in your Christian growth and to whom you can be accountable. Give this person permission to ask you personal questions about your life. Pick someone who loves you enough to be honest with you—to tell you how you really are!

Session THREE

Following Christ

DISCIPLESHIP OBJECTIVE 3:

To experience God's best, you need to follow Christ, serving Jesus as your Lord.

Loosening Up (15-20 minutes)

FOLLOW THE LEADER

Select a leader and spend a few minutes playing Simon Says. After a quick round of Simon Says, discuss these questions:

- How did it feel playing this kids' game?

- Would you rather be the leader or follower? Why?

- Generally speaking, how would you rate yourself on your ability to follow directions?

- How would you rate yourself on following Christ as your leader?

FAITH-BUILDING FOLLOW-UP

Share your experience with last session's Faith-Building Adventure.

Foundation (50-60 minutes)

> If you have a large group, form smaller groups to answer the group discussion questions. Unless otherwise noted, answer the questions in your subgroup. At the end of the Foundation section, allow time for subgroups to report their answers to the whole group.

Jesus Christ wants to be Lord of all in our lives! If you are a Christian, the issue is not whether God lives in you through the Holy Spirit, but whether you are yielding your life to God so that you can experience God's best for you.

Jesus Christ Has the Right to Be Our Lord

1. What are things that typically tend to "rule" our lives?

2. Read the following Scriptures:

• Romans 14:9

• 1 Corinthians 6:20

• Colossians 1:16-18

From these verses, why does Jesus have the right to be our Lord?

What Is Required for Me to Serve Jesus as Lord?

3. Practically, what are ways someone serves Jesus as Lord?

4. Read Luke 9:23-25. What does Jesus say is involved in following him?

5. Practically speaking, giving specific examples, what does it mean to

• deny yourself?

• take up your cross daily?

• follow Christ?

CHARACTERISTICS OF A LORDSHIP DISCIPLE

6. Read Philippians 2:5-11. What attitude did Jesus demonstrate?

7. What are practical everyday ways we can exhibit the attitude of Christ in our lives?

ROADBLOCKS TO CHRIST'S LORDSHIP

8. As you are comfortable sharing, what roadblocks have you experienced in the past that hindered you in serving Christ?

9. What have you found helpful in yielding an area of your life in which you struggle over to God?

Experiencing Christ's Lordship in Your Life

Answer the following questions individually.

10. In evaluating where you are in your relationship with Christ right now, personally reflect on these questions:

• Would you say Christ is Lord of your life? Why or why not?

• What specific area or areas in your life do you need the Holy Spirit to help you yield to Christ?

Spend a couple of minutes in silent prayer.

Taking It to Heart (15-20 minutes)

Key Verses

Form groups of two or three and review the Key Verses for this session:

• Luke 6:46

• Luke 9:23-25

Talking to God

Before closing in prayer, share prayer requests. Be sure to include any updates to requests that were shared in the previous session.

Prayer Requests:

Looking Ahead: The discipleship focus in Session Four is on developing intimacy with God through the practice of a quiet time. As a friendly reminder, between now and the next session you should try and complete this session's Faith-Building Adventure as well as invest time in individual study to prepare for the next session.

Taking It to the House

FAITH-BUILDING ADVENTURE

Between now and the next session, schedule a time to meet with a mature Christian you feel models a lifestyle of serving Jesus as Lord. Interview this person. Before going on your interview, prepare a list of questions to ask, such as

- What would you say is the key to following Jesus?

- What spiritual disciplines (things like prayer and Bible study) do you regularly practice? How do you go about these practices?

- Who has been the most influential person in your spiritual development? What is the best thing that person has done for you?

- What has helped you the most to mature as a Christian?

• When you blow it, how do you get back on track with God?

These are some examples of the kind of questions you might want to ask. Feel free to use these questions, but plan on adding more of your own as well.

PERSONAL PREP FOR SESSION FOUR

You are encouraged to spend approximately ten to fifteen minutes a day over the next week preparing for the next group session.

DAY 1

Key Verses for Session Four

• Mark 1:35

• Philippians 3:10

As you spend time in preparation for Session Four, work on learning one or more of these Key Verses.

Quiet time is a term for spending time alone with God. It's a set, uninterrupted time in your schedule to be with God in order to hear God speak through the Bible, to talk to God in prayer, and to be prepared by the Holy Spirit for the day ahead.

BASICS OF A QUIET TIME

When?

When should I spend time alone with God?

Read the following verses. Write in your own words what these verses say to you.

- Psalm 5:3

_____

_____

- Psalm 55:16-17

_____

_____

- Psalm 119:147-148

_____

_____

- Mark 1:35

_____

_____

These verses are not commands but rather serve as biblical examples. Some people are morning people and some are night owls. The idea is to start the day out with God's blessings and direction. Psychologists say that our pace for the day is set in the first few minutes of the morning. It's harder to stay consistent at night because we are often tired and our other interests compete with our time alone with God. For those of us who fight the "battle of the sheets" each morning, here are some helpful suggestions:

1. Decide on a definite time and place for you to meet with God daily.

2. Guard the hours you need for your sleep: You can't stay up until 1 a.m. each night and expect to be fresh early the next morning to hear God speak to you from the Word of God.

3. Make sure your alarm clock works. (You may need to set it across the room!)

4. When you hear the alarm, *get up*, get dressed and go meet with Jesus.

5. In order to be awake and fresh, you may need to exercise or take a shower before spending time with God. The idea is — *Wake Up!*

DAY 2

Where?

Where should I spend time alone with God?

Read the following verses, recording in your own words the insights you receive.

• Matthew 6:6

_____

_____

• Matthew 14:23

_____

_____

• Luke 4:42

_____

_____

Suggested "Dos and Don'ts":

Don't have your quiet time in bed; it may be *too* quiet! *Do* have your quiet time someplace that is private, where you can be alone and won't be interrupted. And *do* try to meet in the same place and the same time each day (as this practice will help develop spiritual discipline in your life).

How Long?

How much time should I spend in a quiet time?

If you have never had a consistent quiet time, I recommend that you start with just fifteen minutes every morning. The important thing is not the length of time you spend but your *consistency* and the attitude of your heart (we should come to God in *honesty* and *humility*).

DAY 3

What Should I Do?

Divide your quiet time into three five-minute segments focusing on:

• The Bible

• Prayer

• Application

1. Begin with a short prayer, asking God for direction and a teachable spirit.

2. For your first five minutes with God, read the Bible.

3. During the second five minutes, pray.

4. For the final five minutes, take time to meditate and make practical, personal application of what you read in God's Word.

THE BIBLE

Read the following verses, putting into your own words what these verses say to you about God's Word.

- 2 Timothy 3:16-17

Looking ahead: In Session Six we will delve deeper into the topic of the Bible, specifically, Bible study. Here the focus is on incorporating Bible reading into your quiet time.

- Hebrews 4:12

The Bible as Part of Your Quiet Time

Take five minutes to read God's Word during your quiet time before the start of your day.

1. Read the Bible systematically. Set a reading goal. A good one is to read through the Bible once a year. This will help you to see the big picture of what God has done, is doing, and will do. If you average just over three chapters a day, you can read the Bible in a year. But reading a few verses a day is great too! Decide what works best for you and then do it.

2. Write down scriptural insights and ways that you can apply the Bible to your life. Try to make your applications practical, measurable, and obtainable.

DAY 4

Looking ahead: In Session Five we will delve deeper into the topic of prayer. Here the focus is simply on prayer as a component of your quiet time.

PRAYER

During the prayer segment of your quiet time, you may find it helpful to incorporate these five aspects of prayer:

Praise

We need to spend some time every day praising God.

Read the following verses. Write in your own words what they say.

• Psalm 34:1

_____

_____

• Hebrews 13:5

_____

_____

If you would like to read additional verses on praise, scan the book of Psalms.

Praise is our telling God that we think he is _great_! It's an expression of our love for God.

Ways to Praise God:

1. Praise God for his attributes.

Goodness	Knowledge	Wisdom
Mercy	Holiness	Glory
Grace	Love	Additional attributes:
Patience	Power	_____

2. Try reading some of the psalms of praise back to God. Psalm 147 is a good example of a psalm of praise.

3. Or you might want to sing songs of praise to the Lord. Even if you do not sing very well, the Bible says, "Sing to the Lord" (Psalm 98:1) and "Shout for joy to the Lord" (Psalm 100:1). God is more interested in your heart than the quality of your voice.

Confession

Read 1 John 1:9. What does this verse say God will do if we confess our sins?

_____

_____

The word *confession* literally means "to say with"; we are *agreeing with* God that our action was wrong. We should confess sins as we commit them. As we spend time with God, sometimes he will point out areas of sin which we have not noticed. Be sure to thank the Lord for this.

Repentance is not simply feeling sorry about your sin (wrongdoing), but to literally "turn your back on sin" (stop committing the sin). It's changing directions and going God's way. The process of cleansing from sin looks like this:

1. God through the Holy Spirit convicts us.

2. We agree with God that we have done wrong (confess).

3. We choose to do things God's way from now on (repentance).

4. We accept the forgiveness which Jesus provided for us on the cross.

5. We thank God for cleansing us.

6. We demonstrate changed action.

Thanksgiving

Read the following verses. Record what these verses say to you.

• Romans 8:28

_____

_____

• Philippians 4:4

_____

_____

• 1 Thessalonians 5:18

_____

_____

• James 1:2-4

_____

_____

What should a Christian's attitude be regardless of our circumstances? Why should we exhibit such an attitude?

_____

_____

Christians can provide a tremendous example when we give thanks in all situations. We should spend time thanking God for all he has given us, even for the difficult times in life. Most of the time we spend too much time *asking* and too little time *thanking* God. Consider beginning a lifetime habit of thanking God for people, spiritual blessings, physical abilities, good health, materials possession, and character-building problems.

Intercession

Intercession is praying for the needs of other people. It's one of the highest privileges and responsibilities to which God has called Christians. First Samuel 12:23 says, "...far be it from me that I should sin against the Lord by failing to pray for you."

Prayer Requests

God delights in giving things to his children. A request is when we ask God for things that we *need*. Our needs may be spiritual (such as wisdom, love, and patience), mental (such as help to think more clearly or to make a good decision), or physical (such as money, clothes, and physical rest). God doesn't want us to be afraid to ask him for anything. Nothing is too big or too small to ask God for. Philippians 4:6 tells us, "Do not be anxious about anything, but in everything, by prayer and petition, with thanksgiving, present your requests to God."

APPLICATION

Application is the way we can make scriptural insights become a *practical* part of our lives. Using the acrostic **S-P-A-C-E** may help you discover scriptural insights when you are doing your Bible reading.

— Is there a **S**in I need to confess?

— Is there a **P**romise I need to claim?

— Is there an **A**ttitude I need to change?

— Is there a **C**ommand I need to obey?

— Is there an **Example** I need to imitate?

Bonus — Is there anything new that I didn't know before today?

Parting Thought

If you spend just 15 minutes a day with the Lord, that will be 91¼ hours with God a year and 76 days alone with God in 20 years. I pray that you will grow closer and closer to the Lord as you practice spending quiet time with God.

Session FOUR

Developing Intimacy With God

DISCIPLESHIP OBJECTIVE 4:

> To understand and practice the spiritual discipline of spending time alone with God in order to develop a closer relationship with God

Loosening Up (15-20 minutes)

BEST FRIENDS

Begin this session by reflecting on the topic of friendship by discussing the following questions.

• Think about your current best friend or a best friend you had growing up. What about the person you're thinking of made or makes him or her your *best* friend?

• What characteristics or traits do you value the most in a close friend?

• Which characteristics of a close friendship should also be part of a person's relationship with God? Explain.

In Matthew 22:37, Jesus tells us that the greatest commandment is "Love the Lord your God with all your heart and with all your soul and with all your mind." If we are going to grow in a healthy love relationship with anyone, it requires us to spend time getting to know that person. It's hard to love somebody you don't know!

As we work through this session, think about this question: *Am I willing to adjust my schedule in order to spend personal time with God?*

FAITH-BUILDING FOLLOW-UP

Share your experience with last session's Faith-Building Adventure.

Foundation (50-60 minutes)

To grow in our relationship with God, we need to regularly spend time with him. Time that a Christian spends alone with God is sometimes referred to as a quiet time. This time is a set, uninterrupted time in your schedule to be with God in order to hear God speak through the Bible, talk to God in prayer, and be prepared by the Holy Spirit for the day ahead.

BASICS OF A QUIET TIME: WHY? WHEN? WHERE? WHAT?

Why?

1. Read 1 Corinthians 1:9. What does this verse say to you? How would you define the word *fellowship?*

> If you have a large group, form smaller groups to answer the group discussion questions. Unless otherwise noted, answer the questions in your subgroup. At the end of the Foundation section, allow time for subgroups to report their answers to the whole group.

When?

2. What do you generally consider to be your best time of the day? Why?

3. Read the following verses:

• Psalm 5:3

• Psalm 55:16-17

• Psalm 119:147-148

• Mark 1:35

According to these verses, when is a good time to meet with God? What do you think is the key to making a certain time of the day a good time to meet with God?

4. How much of a challenge is it for you to try and spend time alone with God on a regular basis? Explain.

Where?

5. Read the following verses:

• Matthew 6:6

• Mark 6:46

• Luke 4:42

What is important about where a person spends personal time with God?

6. When it comes to spending time alone with God, where do you tend to feel nearest to God?

What? (The Word, Prayer, and Application)

7. When you spend quiet time with God, what things do you generally do as part of this time?

8. Read Matthew 4:4. Why should regularly spending time in God's Word be a part of our lives? What is one way you have benefited from reading the Bible?

9. When it comes to prayer, what is a model or example you have found helpful?

10. What are some practical ways we can apply to our lives what we hear from God when we spend time in prayer and reading the Bible?

Taking It to Heart (15-20 minutes)

KEY VERSES

Form groups of two or three and review the Key Verses for this session:

- Mark 1:35

- Philippians 3:10

Before closing in prayer, share prayer requests. Be sure to include any updates to requests that were shared in the previous session.

Prayer Requests:

Looking Ahead: The discipleship focus in Session Five is prayer. This week be sure to do this session's Faith-Building Adventure as well as spending time in preparation for the next session.

Taking It to the House

FAITH-BUILDING ADVENTURE

This session's adventure is to have a quiet time several times this week (every day, if you can). Set a goal to meet with God a certain number of days over the next week. Work on establishing consistency.

Be realistic. Set aside a specific amount of time. (To start, you may want to plan on fifteen minutes. (Refer to pages 56-62 for a suggested fifteen minute quiet time agenda and ideas for incorporating the Bible, prayer, and application into your quiet time.)

If it would help you to achieve the goal you set, ask a friend to help hold you accountable. Give this person your schedule, and ask him or her to check with you on your progress throughout the week.

PERSONAL PREP FOR SESSION FIVE

Key Verses for Session Five

• John 15:7

• Philippians 4:6-7

Learn these verses before the next session.

Prayer is to be *the* priority for Christians. In Paul's letter of instruction about ministry, he wrote to young Timothy, "I urge, then, first of all, that requests, prayers, intercession and thanksgiving be made for everyone (1 Timothy 2:1)." Oswald Chambers has said, "Prayer does not fit us for the greater works; prayer *is* the greater work." We as ordinary human beings have the ability to change ourselves, our families, our churches, our friends, and our communities from our "prayer closets" because when we enter into true prayer, we touch the heart of God with whom all things are possible. The greatest thing we as Christians can learn to do is *pray*. Did I say learn? Yes. The only way that we learn to pray is by praying. We can go to conferences on prayer, read books about prayer, and hear sermons on prayer, but until we learn to daily come before God ourselves, we will *never* learn the art of prayer.

TWO-WAY COMMUNICATION WITH GOD

Prayer can be looked at as two-way communication with God: Talking and listening.

1. *Talking to God*

Read Matthew 6:9-13. This is one of the most famous prayers in the Bible. Jesus is teaching his disciples how to pray. This prayer has been memorized by many and is often repeated, but I believe its primary purpose is to teach us how to pray specifically.

Reread Matthew 6:9-13. Write down the specific elements of prayer or things to ask that you see in this prayer.

_____

_____

Read the verses that follow. Record what they say to you about prayer.

• Psalm 55:22

_____

_____

• Philippians 4:6-7

_____

_____

• 1 Peter 5:7

_____

_____

2. *Listening to God*

Look up the following verses. For each verse, write in your own words what that verse communicates to you.

• Psalm 5:3

_____

_____

• Isaiah 30:21

_____

_____

• Jeremiah 33:3

_____

_____

DAY 2

Why Pray?

List reasons why you have a difficult time praying.

_____

_____

Look up the following verses. For each verse, write in your own words what each passage says to you.

- Psalm 145:18

- Matthew 7:7-8

- Matthew 18:18-20

- Matthew 26:41

- Mark 1:35

- Luke 21:36

- 1 Thessalonians 5:17

• Hebrews 4:16

_____

_____

• James 5:16

_____

_____

We must remember that the goal of prayer is the ear of God. Unless that is gained the prayer has utterly failed. The utterings of it may have kindled devotional feeling in our minds, the hearing of it may have comforted and strengthened the hearts of those with whom we have prayed, but if the prayer has not gained the heart of God, it has failed in its essential purpose.

—C.H. Spurgeon

DAY 3

How Does God Answer Our Prayers?

For each verse, write what you believe it says regarding the ways God answers prayer and why.

• Mark 14:35-36

_____

_____

• Luke 18:1-8

_____

_____

• 2 Corinthians 12:7-10

_____

_____

• James 5:16-18

_____

_____

• 1 John 5:14-15

_____

_____

Questions About Prayer

Look up the Scripture passages listed in the following chart. Fill in the chart by identifying for each passage: What can be requested, under what conditions, and with what expected result.

	Request	Condition	Result
2 Chronicles 7:14			
John 14:12-14			
John 15:7-8			
John 16:24			
1 John 5:14-15			

Look up the Scripture passages listed in the following chart. Fill in the chart by identifying for each passage: What reason(s) there might be for unanswered prayer and what personal change(s) should take place.

	Reason	Needed Change (make it personal)
Job 35:12-13		
Psalm 66:18		
Psalms 139:23-24		
Matthew 6:33		
Mark 11:25-26		
Ephesians 6:12		
James 1:6-8		
James 4:3		

DAY 5

Promises of God Christians Can Claim Through Prayer

Look up the Scripture passages listed in the following chart. Fill in the chart by identifying for each passage: God's promise and any change you might need to make in your life.

	God's Promise	Change I Need to Make
Isaiah 40:31		
Matthew 6:33		
1 Corinthians 10:13		
2 Corinthians 2:14		
Philippians 4:6-7		
Ephesians 1:3		
James 4:7-8a		
1 John 4:4		
1 John 4:18		
1 John 5:4-5		
1 John 5:18		

Prayer [is] nothing else but a sense of the presence of God.

—Brother Lawrence

Session FIVE

Prayer — Talking and Listening to God

To grow as a Christian you need to understand, learn, and practice the spiritual discipline of prayer.

Loosening Up (15-20 minutes)

CELL PHONE CONNECTION

Standing in a circle, your leader will whisper a message to one of the people next to him or her. Then that message should be repeated (whispered and stated only once) to the next person, and so on until the message makes it back around to the leader. Then discuss the following questions:

• How did the original message compare to the final one?

• What would have made this game easier?

• What are some keys to good communication?

• What would you say are some keys to effective communication with God?

FAITH-BUILDING FOLLOW-UP

Report on your experience with last session's Faith-Building Adventure.

Foundation (50-60 minutes)

WHAT IS PRAYER?

1. Who is someone you admire as a person of prayer? What is it about this person that makes him or her a person of prayer in your eyes?

2. How would you define prayer? Why?

If you have a large group, form smaller groups to answer the group discussion questions. Unless otherwise noted, answer the questions in your subgroup. At the end of the Foundation section, allow time for subgroups to report their answers to the whole group.

3. Read John 14:13-14. What is one goal of prayer?

WHY PRAY?

4. When do you find yourself praying most often?

5. Under what circumstances do you have a hard time praying?

6. Divide the following Scriptures among three or four groups. In your group read your verses and discuss what reasons there are for prayer. After a few minutes, each group should report its insights.

- Psalm 145:18
- Jeremiah 33:3
- Matthew 7:7-8
- Matthew 18:18-20
- Matthew 26:41
- Luke 11:2-4

- Luke 21:36
- Philippians 4:6-7
- 1 Thessalonians 5:17
- Hebrews 4:16
- James 1:5
- James 5:16

How Does God Answer Our Prayers?

7. How many different ways would you say God answers prayer? (If you can, back up your statement with an example—a Bible verse or passage or an example from your own experience.)

8. Read John 15:7 and 1 John 5:14-15. According to these verses, what are some key conditions to prevailing prayer? Practically, how can we meet these conditions in our prayers?

9. What is one way you have experienced the power of prayer in your life?

Promises of God
Christians Can Claim Through Prayer

10. Read the following promises from God:

- Psalm 55:22
- Proverbs 3:5-6
- Isaiah 40:31
- 1 Corinthians 10:13
- Philippians 4:13

- James 4:7-8a
- 1 John 1:9
- 1 John 4:4
- 1 John 4:18
- 1 John 5:4-5

Which Scripture promise (from the list of verses that were just reviewed or from the verses that were looked at for question 6), do you most need to claim in your life right now? Spend a minute in silent prayer.

Taking It to Heart (15-20 minutes)

KEY VERSES

Form groups of two or three and review the Key Verses for this session:

- John 15:7

- Philippians 4:6-7

TALKING TO GOD

Before closing in prayer, share prayer requests. Be sure to include any updates to requests that were shared in the previous session.

Prayer Requests:

Looking Ahead: The discipleship focus in Session Six is the Bible. Come prepared to the next session, having completed the components of the Taking It to the House section.

Taking It to the House

FAITH-BUILDING ADVENTURE

Your application challenge this week is to spend at least some time in prayer everyday this week. One tool that might help you is the following prayer outline divided according to the days of the week:

Sunday—Pray for your church staff and government.

Monday—Pray for your family.

Tuesday—Pray for your close friends.

Wednesday—Pray for your fellow church members.

Thursday—Pray for your neighbors and co-workers.

Friday—Pray for your acquaintances and friends who aren't Christians.

Saturday—Pray for non-Christians and the opportunity to tell them about Jesus.

You may also find it beneficial while exploring the topic of prayer to find a mature Christian (a senior at your church) who likes to pray. Ask this person why he or she likes to pray and how prayer has benefited his or her life. Ask your "prayer person" if you can pray together. You may want to team up with another person or couple in this group to meet and pray with the person of prayer that you identify. Remember, the Bible says, "For where two or three come together in my name, there am I with them" (Matthew 18:20).

DAY 1

Key Verses for Session Six

• 2 Timothy 3:16-17

• Hebrews 4:12

Learn these verses for Session Six.

Why Study the Bible?

Look up the following verses. For each verse write in your own words why you should study the Bible.

• Joshua 1:8

_____

_____

• Psalm 1:1-3

_____

_____

• Psalm 119:11

_____

_____

• Psalm 119:105

_____

_____

- Acts 17:11

- Romans 10:17

- Ephesians 6:17

- Colossians 3:16

- 2 Timothy 2:15

- 2 Timothy 3:14-17

- Hebrews 4:12

Dr. Joe Heacock, a retired seminary professor, once said that students of the Bible are "Spiritual surgeons who are operating with eternal consequences in the balance."

DAY 2

Bible Study Tools

You need the proper biblical *surgical instruments* if you are planning to operate successfully for eternal results. If you do not have these instruments, begin to collect them. Ask your family and friends to give them to you as gifts for your birthday and for Christmas. You may also want to check with your pastor and at your church library and Christian bookstore. For the study tools you don't have, there's no need to go out and buy all these tools at once. Rather, as you study and find the enjoyment and value of each tool, begin collecting these tools to build your personal Bible study library.

Bibles. Have copies of various modern translations such as The New International Version, the New American Standard Bible, the New Living Translation, and the New King James Version. This will give you multiple translations to study a particular passage. You need more than one translation to study the Bible effectively. There are also parallel Bibles available — Bibles that include multiple translations side by side.

There are also a number of excellent study Bibles on the market. A good study Bible (or two) is a wise investment for the serious student of the Bible. Within a study Bible, there are features such as study notes, maps, and a concordance. Some study Bibles I would recommend are *The NIV (New International Version) Study Bible*; *The Thompson Chain-Reference Bible*; *Life Application Study Bible*; *Ryrie Study Bible*; *Disciple's Study Bible*; *African American Jubilee Edition Bible*; *The Discovery Bible*; *The Open Bible*; and *Nave's Study Bible,* to name several.

Notebook. Keep your Bible study notes in a notebook.

Bible dictionary. Use a Bible dictionary, which provides an alphabetical listing of biblical terms and names with information as to their meaning (such as *Unger's Bible Dictionary*).

Concordance. To allow you to find where and how terms are used, try a concordance. It contains an alphabetical list of the principal words of the Bible. Some good ones that I recommend are *Cruden's Complete Concordance, Strong's Exhaustive Concordance,* and *Young's Analytical Concordance to the Bible.*

Bible atlas. Keep a Bible atlas on hand in order to refer to the collection of maps that identify locations where most historical events in the Bible took place.

Commentaries. Consult a Bible commentary for an interpretation and explanation of biblical passages.

English grammar book. Check a grammar book to help you identify the various parts of speech.

Dictionary. To help you to define words that you don't know, look up the words in a dictionary.

Additional helps. Try Bible study books, like this course, and other books on Bible study methods.

Which of the above tools do you already have?

_____

_____

Which of these tools would you like to acquire in the near future?

_____

_____

Read and study Philippians 3:10. Try to use as many of the different "surgical instruments" as you can in your study of this verse.

Four Types of Bible Study

One of the rich experiences of the Christian life is when God through the Holy Spirit begins to open to us the treasures of the Bible. Here are four kinds of Bible study that can help you discover these treasures.

Character Study

1. Select a character in the Bible to study—Moses, Joseph, Deborah, David, Mary, Peter, Paul, or Lydia, for example.

2. Write down as much biographical data as you can find—family information, where your character was from, where your character lived, and facts like this.

3. List all the passages you can find that relate to the character you are studying.

4. Make a list of the major events in your character's life.

5. Make a list of both positive and negative characteristics.

6. Write down three things that you learned from studying this person's life.

7. Write down any common characteristics, positive or negative, you have with the person you are studying.

8. Ask yourself what you can do to maintain or improve your positive characteristics and what you can do to lessen or eliminate your negative characteristics.

Devotional Study

1. Read a Bible passage and write down things to help you, such as a simple outline, basic content, and the speaker and audience.

2. Write down the *key* idea of the passage in one sentence.

3. Track cross-references, and look up and write down related passages.

4. Record a personal application for your life for *today*!

Topical Study

1. Select a topic such as faith, serving others, giving, or love—really anything that you are interested in what the Bible has to say about it.

2. Research verses relating to the topic by using a concordance.

3. List key verses and summarize these in your own words.

4. Pick out verses that have special significance to you.

5. Summarize thoughts about the topic.

Book of the Bible

1. Choose a book of the Bible you are interested in studying in depth.

2. Break the book into sections to study by verses, passages, outlines, and chapters.

3. Collect outside sources (for example, a commentary on the book you are studying) that you feel would be helpful in your study.

4. Record the key themes, passages, teachings, and characters.

A Method for Bible Study

The following information outlines an approach you can take in studying the Bible. This approach may be applied regardless of the type of Bible study (character, devotional, topical, book of the Bible, or other) you are doing.

Basic Guidelines

1. Select a plan of study and stick with it.

2. Study at your own pace. Try to be consistent with your time each week for your Bible study in the amount of time you study as well as your starting time. But be careful not to put yourself through a guilt trip while you are trying to grow deeper spiritually.

3. Ask God to make Psalm 119:18 a reality as you study.

4. Give the Holy Spirit permission to make changes to your life according to God's Word.

5. Study primarily for personal application.

6. Write down your new commitments in your Bible study notebook.

Observation

Read your passage of Scripture with a pen and notebook close by, summarizing and outlining as you study the text.

Steps in observation:

Step 1: Prayerfully read the text. Be open-minded as you read so that you may receive what God wants to teach you, and with a humble heart so that you will obey God's Word.

Step 2: Thoughtfully observe. As you read, see what the text is saying and its meaning. Concentration is critical.

Step 3: Deliberately observing the text, concentrate on words and phrases. Ask and answer these questions: Who? What? When? Where? Why? and How? The most effective way to study is to write down what you observe and your questions.

Practice the steps of observation: Study Hebrews 4:12, recording your observation in the space that follows:

Interpretation

1. Ask the question: "What did the author mean?" Do this in context of the setting of the text, which requires studying the verses before and after and possibly the preceding and following chapters.

2. Use an accurate translation of the Bible.

3. Use good Bible and English dictionaries to define unknown words. Incorporate the definitions into the text for a better understanding.

4. Use other Bible aids when needed, such as atlases, concordances, and commentaries.

5. Summarize the primary message of the text.

Personal Application

1. Write how this text applies to your life. Have you lived (or not lived) in knowing or unknowing compliance to this text? What have been the results and the consequences?

2. Look for actions, attitudes, challenges, commands, examples, promises, sins, skills, and warnings.

3. Be specific.

4. Be personal. Use the personal pronouns "I," or "me," instead of "all Christians should" or "we can't." For example, you can begin sentences with "I need to…"

5. Be practical. One example might be "I need to love my spouse by cleaning our bedroom."

6. Make goals measurable and obtainable: "I need to love my spouse by cleaning our bedroom this Saturday morning."

7. Create a way you can share this new truth with a friend.

Memorization

Pick the most meaningful verses from the text and memorize them. If you have difficulty learning self-selected verses, I recommend that you consider purchasing some kind of topical memory system. Check with your local Christian bookstore to see what resources are available.

As we put God's Word in our hearts through memorization, we become more *effective* in our Christian walks. When Jesus was being tempted in the wilderness, he fought off the attacks of Satan by quoting Scripture. Also, we become much more effective in sharing our faith when we have many needed Scripture verses at a thought's command.

Some practical steps for memorizing Scripture:

1. *Read the verse several times aloud.* This will help you understand the verse. Reading aloud helps you to memorize the verse more quickly. The more senses you use the better your ability to memorize.

2. *Comprehend the verse.* This will help you to use the verse correctly.

• Read the verse in the *context* of the chapter and book it is in. This is done by reading the verses before and after it.

• If possible, read about this verse in a Bible commentary.

• Discover the main topic of the verse.

3. *Divide the verse into natural phrases.* Use commas in the verse as natural breaks.

4. *Learn the reference as part of the verse.* This will help you be able to locate the verse in your mind and in the Bible. It will also help the one with whom you share the verse be able to find it. Say the reference before and after the verse.

5. *Learn to say the verse word perfect.* It's just as easy to learn the verse the right way as it is the wrong way. If you share the verse with others and they find out you quoted it incorrectly, it may impact your credibility with them.

6. *Apply the verse to your life.* Pray, asking God to show you how this verse can affect your life for God's glory. When the verse is a part of you, and not just words, you will never forget it.

7. *Review the verse systematically!* This helps cement the verse in your

mind forever. Choose one day of the week to review the verses that you are learning. If you review a verse for thirty days, you are unlikely to forget it. If you have a non-Christian friend at work or in your neighborhood, have your friend check you as you recite your verses.

8. *Remember: Memorizing Scripture takes discipline!* But also remember, "...my word that goes out from my mouth: It will not return to me empty" (Isaiah 55:11).

DAY 5

Applying Truth to Your Life

You are now ready for "surgery." Apply the steps of observation, interpretation, application, and memorization to James 1:23-25. Do each step carefully.

Parting Thought

While your biblical knowledge will increase as a result of studying the Bible, keep in mind that the primary purpose of the Bible is to be a *life-changing* book. As good as it is to learn more about the Bible, be careful to approach your study of God's Word with the right motivation: a desire to apply its truth to your life.

Session SIX

Bible Study—Digging Deeper

DISCIPLESHIP OBJECTIVE 6:

Gaining a deeper understanding of God's will for your life begins by learning how to effectively study the Bible for yourself.

Loosening Up (15-20 minutes)

THE GOOD BOOK

Start this session by picking one or two of the following questions to answer and share with the group.

• Other than the Bible, what is a book you really like. Why?

• When did you first start reading the Bible on your own? Why?

• From the Bible, what is your favorite Bible story? book of the Bible? Bible character? Bible passage or verse? Explain.

FAITH-BUILDING FOLLOW-UP

Report on your experience with last session's Faith-Building Adventure.

Foundation (50-60 minutes)

If you have a large group, form smaller groups to answer the group discussion questions. Unless otherwise noted, answer the questions in your subgroup. At the end of the Foundation section, allow time for subgroups to report their answers to the whole group.

The Word of God is indispensable to the life of a Christian, just as blood flowing through our physical bodies is indispensable for physical life.

WHY STUDY THE BIBLE?

1. What would you say is the main reason you study the Bible?

2. What are the benefits of studying the Bible? In two minutes, try to come up with as many ways you can think of (have someone keep time and someone write). Then from your list of benefits, narrow it down to the top five.

3. Divide the following verses between two groups:

- Joshua 1:8
- Psalm 1:1-3
- Psalm 119:11
- Acts 17:11
- 2 Timothy 2:15
- 2 Timothy 3:14-17
- Hebrews 4:12

Discuss in your group what your verses say about Scripture. Specifically, for each of your passages, what is required of us in relation to Scripture and what is the subsequent benefit or reward?

BIBLE STUDY TOOLS

4. Who is someone who has helped you to better understand and appreciate the Bible?

5. What Bible study tools have you found most helpful to you in your study of God's Word?

TYPES OF BIBLE STUDY

6. What types of Bible study have you done on your own? Of the four types of Bible study outlined in the personal preparation section for this session (pp. 87-88)—character, devotional, topical, or book of the Bible—which interests you the most? Why?

APPLYING TRUTH TO YOUR LIFE

7. In the personal preparation section for this session, a method of Bible study was presented (pp. 89-93) that included these components:

- Observation

- Interpretation

- Personal application

- Memorization

Discuss what is involved in applying these components to the study of Scripture. Now apply these steps to 2 Timothy 3:16-17.

8. Read James 1:23-25. What is the difference between a hearer of the Word and a doer of the Word?

9. Read Matthew 4:1-11. How did Jesus use his knowledge of

Scripture? Now read Psalm 119:11 and 1 Peter 3:15. What other benefits are there to having Scripture committed to memory?

10. What is one way the Bible has influenced your life?

Taking It to Heart (15-20 minutes)

KEY VERSES

Form groups of two or three and review the Key Verses for this session:

- 2 Timothy 3:16-17

- Hebrews 4:12

TALKING TO GOD

Before closing in prayer, share prayer requests. Be sure to include any updates to requests that were shared in the previous session.

Prayer Requests:

Looking Ahead: The discipleship focus in the next session is on the Holy Spirit. If you have been faithful to complete the Taking It to the House section of each session, that's great — *way to go!* You are halfway through. Keep it up! However, even if you haven't been doing the application and preparation components of this study, it's not too late to start. Why not commit yourself to that as an action step this week? I believe you will be glad you did.

Taking It to the House

FAITH-BUILDING ADVENTURE

This week's adventure is a challenge to move beyond Bible reading into Bible study.

• Set a time (or times) you would like to schedule to study the Bible this week: _____

• Select the place where you will study the Bible: _____

• Choose the type of study you would like to do (see the list of four types of Bible study outlined on pages 87-88): _____

When you spend time studying the Bible, work to apply the method for Bible study as outlined on pages 89-93. Remember, start slow. Make a plan and stick to it. Study at a pace that is comfortable for you. Be consistent, and keep in mind the ultimate goal of Bible study is to apply the truth of God's Word to your life.

Key Verses for Session Seven

- Galatians 2:20

- Ephesians 5:17-18

Who Is the Holy Spirit?

Look up the following verses. For each verse, write in your own words what it says to you about who the Holy Spirit is.

- Matthew 28:19

_____

_____

- John 14:16-17

_____

_____

- John 15:26

_____

_____

- John 16:13-15

_____

_____

DAY 2

The Trinity

Look up the following verses and write what these verses say to you about the relationship between the Holy Spirit and God and Jesus.

- Matthew 3:16-17

_____

_____

- Mark 1:9-11

_____

_____

- Luke 3:21-22

_____

_____

- 1 Corinthians 6:11

_____

_____

- 2 Corinthians 13:14

_____

_____

For the following verses, record how you see the Holy Spirit at work with Jesus during his time on earth.

- Luke 4:1

- Luke 4:14-19

- John 1:32-34

- Romans 8:11

What the Holy Spirit Does

Look up the following verses. For each passage, write in your own words what it says to you about what the Holy Spirit does.

- John 14:25-27

- John 16:7-8

- John 16:13-14

- Acts 1:8

- Romans 8:1-2

- Romans 8:9

- Romans 8:15-17

- Romans 8:26-27

- Ephesians 1:13-14

DAY 4

Not Living by the Spirit

Read Romans 8:5-17 and Galatians 5:15-26. List what actions, acts, and attitudes characterize our sinful nature.

_____

_____

_____

_____

Reviewing your list, take a few minutes to prayerfully reflect on this question: How do I see these things in my life?

_____

_____

Life by the Spirit

Revisit Romans 8:5-17 and Galatians 5:15-26. Record what actions, acts, and attitudes characterize living by the Spirit.

_____

_____

_____

_____

Reviewing your list, take a few minutes to prayerfully reflect on this question: How do I see these things in my life?

_____

_____

DAY 5

Grieving the Holy Spirit

When we try to live our life in our own power, we sin and grieve the Holy Spirit.

Read Ephesians 4:31–5:11. Record what actions grieve the Holy Spirit.

_____

_____

_____

_____

So, what should a Christian who has sinned do to restore fellowship with Christ? Do we have a quiet time seven days in a row? Do we become more active in church? Do we memorize more Bible verses?

Even though these are good things in themselves, doing them to try and change the heart of God or to excuse our sin is wrong. We can do nothing apart from God to gain forgiveness for our sin. Rather, we should yield ourselves to God and the Holy Spirit.

Yielding to the Holy Spirit

Ephesians 5:18 instructs us to "be filled with the Spirit." The key to living by the Spirit is being *filled* (controlled) with (by) the Holy Spirit.

As you complete your preparation for the upcoming session, ask God to walk with you and empower you through the Holy Spirit.

1. *Understand* that the Holy Spirit lives inside you because you are a Christian. Galatians 4:6 tells us, "Because you are sons [and daughters], God sent the Spirit of his Son into our hearts, the Spirit who calls out, '*Abba [Daddy]*, Father.' "

2. *Consider* that God desires that you yield completely to the Holy Spirit. This is how you experience the abundant life mentioned in John 10:10.

3. *Repent* of any sin in your life. To *repent* literally means to turn your back on the sin and stop doing the sin. It does not mean to feel sorry for your sin and then continue to repeat it. Repentance should follow confession. Confession is saying we agree with God that our sin is wrong. See 1 John 1:9.

4. *Reject* sinful desires which keep you from experiencing God's best. Pray for Galatians 2:20 to be a consistent reality in your life.

5. *Yield* to the Holy Spirit. You received the Holy Spirit by faith and so continue to live by faith in relationship to the Holy Spirit. "So I say, live by the Spirit, and you will not gratify the desires of the sinful nature…Since we live by the Spirit, let us keep in step with the Spirit" (Galatians 5:16, 25).

6. *Enjoy* the blessings of the Holy Spirit in your life.

Look up the following passages, recording the blessings that come from the Holy Spirit:

• John 15:5-11

_____

_____

• Galatians 5:22-25

_____

_____

Write a prayer, asking God to empower you to yield totally to the leading of the Holy Spirit in your life.

_____

_____

_____

_____

_____

_____

_____

Session SEVEN

The Holy Spirit and You

To gain a better understanding of the Holy Spirit and what the Holy Spirit can do in your life.

Loosening Up (15-20 minutes)

LOOKING FOR SOME DIRECTION

> **Leader:** For this Loosening Up activity, you will need to make sure you have several sheets of paper. Also, before doing this activity, you need to create a simple drawing of basic geometric shapes that touch or intersect like the sample illustration on page 159.

Have everyone in the group pair up with a partner and sit back to back in such a way that one person in each pair is facing the leader and the other is not. Each person facing away from the leader will be a designated "artist"; the artists will need paper and pen. Each person facing the leader will be a "describer."

Once everyone is situated, the leader will show the describers a picture, and in turn the describers will tell the artists what to draw. You have two minutes to work with your partner to complete this task. After time is called, artists can turn around and see what they were supposed to be drawing. Compare drawings, then discuss these questions:

• What made this activity difficult? easy?

• How did you feel about your partner as you worked together?

• Briefly describe a time someone had to guide you so you could accomplish a task or reach a goal. How did that feel?

FAITH-BUILDING FOLLOW-UP

Report on your experience with last session's Faith-Building Adventure.

Foundation (50-60 minutes)

THE HOLY SPIRIT

1. How would you explain to a friend who the Holy Spirit is?

> If you have a large group, form smaller groups to answer the group discussion questions. Unless otherwise noted, answer the questions in your subgroup. At the end of the Foundation section, allow time for subgroups to report their answers to the whole group.

2. How would you characterize the relationship between God, Jesus, and the Holy Spirit?

3. In groups of two or three, divide up the following Scriptures. In your group read your verses and discuss what your Bible passages say about the role of the Holy Spirit in your lives. Then take turns reporting your insights to the larger group.

- Matthew 28:19
- John 14:16
- John 15:26
- John 14:16-17

- John 16:13-15
- Acts 1:8
- Romans 8:1-2
- Romans 8:9

- Romans 8:15-17
- Romans 8:26-27
- Ephesians 1:13-14
- 1 John 4:13-18

4. If you were writing a job description for the Holy Spirit based on the passages we discussed, what might the description include?

5. Which of the roles the Holy Spirit wants to play in your life do you need or appreciate the most right now? Why?

How Should We Live?

6. Form two groups, with each group taking one of the following passages:

- Romans 8:5-17

- Galatians 5:15-26

Read your passage and compare and contrast life by the Spirit versus life by the sinful nature. What are the differences? After a few minutes, share and compare your findings.

7. What are the consequences or results of living according to the sinful nature? living according to the Spirit?

Yielding to the Spirit

8. Read John 15:1-11. What is required in order to live a life yielded to the Holy Spirit? Practically, how can we do this?

9. Read Galatians 5:22-25 again. What specific blessings come from living by the Spirit? What is the key to experiencing the fruit of the Spirit in your life?

10. Spend a quiet moment thinking about your day. Have you displayed the fruit of the Spirit in your actions and attitudes? Is there any pruning God needs to do so you can consistently allow the Holy Spirit to work in your life? Prayerfully reflect in silence for a few minutes about what those things might be.

Taking It to Heart (15-20 minutes)

KEY VERSES

Form groups of two or three and review the Key Verses for this session:

- Galatians 2:20

- Ephesians 5:17-18

TALKING TO GOD

Before closing in prayer, share prayer requests. Be sure to include any updates to requests that were shared in the previous session.

Prayer Requests:

Looking Ahead: The discipleship focus in the next session is spiritual warfare. Come prepared to the next session, having completed the components of the Taking It to the House section.

Taking It to the House

FAITH-BUILDING ADVENTURE

In Ephesians 5:18 Paul encourages us to "be filled with the Spirit." The key to letting the Holy Spirit impact our actions and attitudes is to be filled with the Holy Spirit.

We discovered that the Holy Spirit wants to work in and through us in many ways. This coming week look for the Holy Spirit to be at work daily in your world.

Monday

Read John 14:16-17.

Jesus says the Holy Spirit will be our *paraclete*, which is translated as *counselor*. The Greek term *paraclete* means counselor and a whole lot more, including helper, comforter, and teacher. In what ways did the Holy Spirit comfort you today?

Tuesday

Read John 16:12-15.

The Holy Spirit wants to lead us to understanding the truth about Jesus and God. In what way did your knowledge of God and faith deepen today?

Wednesday

Read Acts 1:4-9.

The Holy Spirit brought power into the lives of Jesus' disciples. The Holy Spirit helps believers lead powerful, God-honoring lives. In what ways did you see the Holy Spirit bring power into your life today?

Thursday

Read Romans 8:1-2.

Many people lead lives of guilt and shame. But because of Jesus' sacrifice, we're free from relying on our own goodness to please God. The Holy Spirit helps us experience the freedom of being new in Christ.

In what way did you experience the reality of God's grace today?

_____

_____

Friday

Read Romans 8:8-9; 15-17.

The Holy Spirit reminds us that we belong to Jesus. In what way today did you experience the joy of being a child of God through Jesus Christ?

_____

_____

Saturday

Read Ephesians 1:13-14.

The Holy Spirit is in a way a "down payment," preparing us for the day when we'll be with God. In what ways today were you reminded of what it's like to be with God?

_____

_____

Sunday

Read 1 John 4:13-18.

God is love, and the Holy Spirit wants you to know God ever more intimately. In what way today did you feel God's love?

_____

_____

Key Verses for Session Eight

- 1 Peter 5:8-9

- 1 John 4:4

Work on learning these verses by the next session.

The Battle Zone

- Read Ephesians 6:12. Where are some of the evil forces located?

_____

_____

- Read Daniel 10:1-14. What is going on with Daniel and the answer to his prayer?

_____

_____

- Read Job 1:6 and Job 2:1-2. Where is Satan when he is talking to God? Where had Satan been?

_____

_____

- Read Revelation 20:7-10. What ultimately becomes of Satan?

_____

_____

DAY 2

Names of Our Enemy

For the following Scriptures, identify the various names by which our enemy is called (you may want to consult various Bible versions).

- Genesis 3:4 _____
- Matthew 12:24 _____
- Matthew 13:19 _____
- Luke 10:18 _____
- John 8:44 _____
- John 14:30 _____
- 2 Corinthians 4:4 _____

- 2 Corinthians 6:15 _____
- 2 Corinthians 11:14 _____
- Ephesians 2:2 _____
- 1 Thessalonians 3:5 _____
- Revelation 9:11 _____
- Revelation 12:10 _____
- Revelation 20:2 _____

DAY 3

Satan's Origin

Record in your own words what these verses say about Satan.

- Isaiah 14:12-14

_____

_____

- Ezekiel 28:14-17

_____

_____

- Revelation 12:7-9

_____

_____

Characteristics of Satan

For the following verses, record the characteristics of Satan that you identify (some characteristics may be implied):

- Genesis 3:1-4 _____

- Job 1:6-11 _____

- John 8:44 _____

- 2 Corinthians 11:3 _____

- 2 Corinthians 11:14 _____

- Ephesians 2:2 _____

- 1 Timothy 3:6-7 _____

- 1 Peter 5:8-9 _____

DAY 4

Satan's Power

Look up these verses, writing in your own words what they say to you about Satan's power.

- Matthew 25:41-43

_____

_____

- Luke 22:3-4

_____

_____

- John 8:42-44

_____

_____

• Acts 13:8-10

_____

_____

• 2 Corinthians 4:3-4

_____

_____

• Ephesians 2:1-3

_____

_____

• 2 Thessalonians 2:9-10a

_____

_____

• 1 John 3:10

_____

_____

Tactics Satan Uses to Attack

Look up the following Scripture passages and record the tactics you identify.

• Genesis 3:1 _____

• 1 Chronicles 21:1 _____

• Job 2:7 _____

• Zechariah 3:1 _____

• Matthew 4:5-6 _____

- Matthew 4:8-9 _____

- Luke 22:31 _____

- 2 Corinthians 11:3 _____

Satan's Deceptions

1. You should be able to do miracles on demand.

2. You receive power in words through spells and witchcraft.

3. Seek personal experiences of demonic influence, out-of-body experiences, visions, and hearing audible "voices."

4. You can become a god.

5. Remember that faith equals sight.

6. Seek wealth, health, and power.

7. You can have heaven here on earth.

8. You can accomplish great things with Satan's help.

Satan Maximizes	God Emphasizes
1. the temporal	1. the eternal
2. immediate pleasure	2. long-term rewards
3. momentary feeling	3. lasting effect
4. having fun now!	4. the cost later!

God's Power to Overcome Satan

Read the verses that follow, noting the power God gives Christians.

• Psalm 119:11, 105

_____

_____

• Matthew 18:18-20

_____

_____

• John 14:12-14

_____

_____

• 1 Corinthians 10:13

_____

_____

• 2 Corinthians 2:10-11

_____

_____

• Ephesians 6:10-18

_____

_____

• 2 Thessalonians 3:2-3

_____

_____

- James 4:7-8a

- 1 Peter 5:8-9

- 1 John 2:12-14

- Revelation 12:10-11

A Word of Caution

Read Acts 19:13-16. What can happen to those trying to find demons to cast out?

Make sure the same doesn't happen to you. Don't go chasing the devil. When God wants you to have an encounter or when you are spiritually ready for such an encounter, the devil or demons will come to you.

Session EIGHT

Knowing Your Enemy

To identify your enemy and to recognize the means
you have in Christ to resist Satan.

Loosening Up (15-20 minutes)

"GIVE ME YOUR LUNCH MONEY, OR ELSE!"

Begin this session by thinking back to your school days. Choose one
or two of the following questions to answer and share with the group.

• When was a time you were picked on or harassed by a bully?
Describe the circumstances.

• If there was a bully in your life, what things did you do to keep
the bully from bothering you? How successful were your efforts?

• What common characteristics do you think bullies share?

• What advice would you give a child who's dealing with a school-
yard bully?

FAITH-BUILDING FOLLOW-UP

Report on your experience with last session's Faith-Building
Adventure.

Foundation (50-60 minutes)

The purpose of this session is *not* for us to dwell on Satan and his
power. Rather, it's to make us aware of who our enemy is and the power
we have through Jesus Christ. We don't need to fear Satan, but we
should have a healthy respect for him and an awareness of his evil tactics. Christ has won the war; we don't need to lose unnecessary battles.

The Battle

1. When you hear the phrase *spiritual warfare*, what thoughts or images come to mind?

If you have a large group, form smaller groups to answer the group discussion questions. Unless otherwise noted, answer the questions in your subgroup. At the end of the Foundation section, allow time for subgroups to report their answers to the whole group.

2. According to Ephesians 6:10-12, who is our struggle against? How would you classify the kind of struggle we are in? What are the stakes?

3. Read Deuteronomy 18:9-13. What additional forms do practices like these take today? Why should such activities be avoided?

Know Your Enemy

In up to four separate subgroups, have each group look at one or more of the following "Know Your Enemy" sections (questions 4a-4d), then report your findings and conclusions back to the larger group.

Know Your Enemy — by Name

4a. Read the following passages, noting the names given to Satan.

- John 14:28-31

- 2 Corinthians 11:14

- 1 Thessalonians 3:5

• Revelation 12:10

How do these names for Satan reflect on his character and the roles he tries to play in our lives?

Know Your Enemy — by Strength

4b. Read the following passages, noting the limitations of Satan's power.

• Mark 5:1-13

• Acts 13:6-12

• Ephesians 2:1-4

• 1 John 4:4

How powerful is Satan? How is this power limited?

Know Your Enemy — by Tactic

4c. Read the following passages, noting how Satan goes about doing evil in the world.

• Genesis 3:1 and 2 Corinthians 11:3

• Job 2:7 and Luke 22:31

• Zechariah 3:1

• Matthew 4:5-7

What tactics do you think Satan finds especially effective in your community?

Know Your Enemy—the Battleground

4d. Read the following passages, noting where Satan goes to do evil.

• Job 1:7; 2:1-2

• Ephesians 2:1-2

• Ephesians 6:12

• 1 Peter 5:8-9

What are specific ways you see Satan active in the world?

DEFEAT YOUR ENEMY—BY CHRIST'S POWER

5. Read the following passages, noting how in Jesus we can find help confronting Satan's evil.

• 1 Corinthians 10:13

• 2 Corinthians 2:10-11

• Ephesians 6:10-18

What weapons are available to us in our spiritual battle? Which of these are offensive weapons? defensive weapons? What are practical ways we can use these tools?

6. In regard to the means available to us to resist or overcome Satan, what resource do you appreciate the most? Why?

7. Read Matthew 4:1-11. How did Satan attack Jesus? How did Jesus rebuff Satan's attacks? How can we apply this tactic?

8. Read Acts 19:13-16. What lessons about engaging in a spiritual battle do you see in this passage? Explain.

Taking It to Heart (15-20 minutes)

KEY VERSES

Form groups of two or three and review the Key Verses for this session:

- 1 Peter 5:8-9

- 1 John 4:4

TALKING TO GOD

Before closing in prayer, share prayer requests. Be sure to include any updates to requests that were shared in the previous session.

Prayer Requests:

Looking Ahead: The discipleship focus in Session Nine is on treating everyone, regardless of cultural or racial differences, the way Jesus would. Come prepared to the next session having completed the components of the Taking It to the House section.

Taking It to the House

FAITH-BUILDING ADVENTURE

This week you and your Bible will make a field trip to your local video rental outlet. When you have time to browse, stop by the video store and visit the horror section.

You're not there to rent a video. Rather, you're there to pray.

Walk the aisles and glance at the video covers. See how many videos are there. Our culture has a fascination with the supernatural and an almost tragic misunderstanding of Satan and evil. Some videos present Satan as an all-powerful being; others, as an almost comic figure. As you discovered in this week's study, both representations are lies.

Satan is not all-powerful. In fact, his total defeat is assured through the power of God. But Satan is also not a pitchfork-carrying horned caricature. He's real and so is spiritual warfare.

Step away from the horror section, open your Bible, and read Romans 8:31-39. How does reading this make you feel?

Read this passage again. How much does God love you?

Read this passage again. How powerful is the God who loves you?

Read this passage again. How far can Satan separate you from God?

Read this passage once more. How secure are you in God's love?

Bonus challenge: Over the course of your regular activities this week, work to be intentionally sensitive to the spiritual battle that is going on all around you. Then when you run across the things of Satan, make it a point to stop and pray.

PERSONAL PREP FOR SESSION NINE

DAY 1

Key Verses for Session Nine

• 1 Samuel 16:7

• 1 John 4:20-21

As you spend time preparing for Session Nine, work on learning these Key Verses. Try and commit to memory at least one of these passages.

American Christianity seems to have at least two divisive flaws: prejudging others and the inability of knowing how to love people, in or out of the church, that we don't like. We may agree intellectually and theologically that it's wrong to prejudge and to not show love to everyone, but too often there's a gap between our mental acceptance of these principles and our practical application of them.

What Is Prejudging?

• Write in your own words what you would say prejudging is.

_____

_____

• Look up the word _prejudge_ or _prejudice_ in a dictionary. Record that definition here:

_____

_____

• Think of a situation where you felt you were prejudged. Jot down a few notes about what happened.

_____

_____

• Think of a time when you have been guilty of prejudging. Briefly outline what happened.

_____

_____

DAY 2

Examples of Prejudging

Prejudging happened in the Bible! Can you believe it? Following are five examples of prejudging or prejudice. Read each account, and then record your observations about the bases for these judgments. (Mark these passages, as you will be revisiting these same chapters shortly.)

• Numbers 12:1-2 (In addition to looking up this passage, look up Cushitic or Cushite in a dictionary and a Bible dictionary.)

_____

_____

• 1 Samuel 16:1-10

_____

_____

• Luke 10:30-35

_____

_____

• John 1:43-46

_____

_____

• James 2:1-4

_____

_____

The Right Response to Being Prejudged

Now let's look at the "conclusion" to the examples of prejudging you just looked at. This time, focus on the response, result, or lesson you see in the following passages. Record your insights.

• Numbers 12:4-13

_____

_____

• 1 Samuel 16:11-13

_____

_____

• Luke 10:36-37

_____

_____

• John 1:47-49

_____

_____

• James 2:8-9

_____

_____

DAY 3

Following Jesus' Steps

In John 4, Jesus develops a relationship with someone of a different culture. Read John 4:1-42. Identify as many steps as you can (some may be implied) that Jesus took to develop this relationship.

• Step 1: _____

_____

_____

_____

_____

_____

DAY 4

Loving People You Don't Like!

If we are honest, we must admit that, even as Christians, there are people that we don't like. I'm not just talking about people we don't know personally and don't like (certain politicians and celebrities, for example); rather, I'm referring to the people we personally know—people from church, work, the neighborhood, or the fitness club—who tend to rub us the wrong way. There's no doubt these people exist. However, as Christians, we are called to love *everyone*!

Look up the following verses. Write in your own words the points these passages communicate to you.

• Matthew 5:43-48

_____

_____

• Luke 6:35-36

_____

_____

- John 13:34-35

- John 15:12-14

- Romans 12:9-10

- Romans 13:8-10

- Ephesians 5:1-2

- 1 John 3:16

- 1 John 4:7

• 1 John 4:19-21

_____

_____

DAY 5

Moving Toward Love Through Forgiveness

1. Make a list of people with whom you have an open or ongoing conflict, including a brief description of the problem.

_____

_____

_____

_____

_____

Don't share this list. This is confidential between you and Christ.

2. Read Matthew 6:14-15 and Mark 11:25. Write down in your own words what these verses say.

_____

_____

3. Pray over your list. Ask God to help you forgive the people you identified. Pray a prayer of forgiveness for them now.

4. Plan to pray for the people on your list on a regular basis. If you have a prayer list or journal, add their names to this now. It's difficult to continue disliking someone for whom you pray regularly.

5. Read Romans 12:14-21. What does this passage tell us to do for the people who hurt us?

_____

_____

You will find *freedom* from emotional bondage to people who have hurt you by asking God to *bless* them. This may not make sense, but it works. God's ways are higher that ours (Isaiah 55:8-9).

If you don't forgive those who have hurt you, they will continue to own you. Whenever you see the person who hurt you, the hurt and emotion returns, as if the incident just happened. Any person who falls into this scenario is, in a sense, "owned" by the other person. The person who hurt the other gains control every time the two interact (it can even occur by just seeing the person). This is a type of mental slavery.

If you forgive someone who has wounded you, it doesn't mean that you will become best friends or should become best friends; but forgiveness is the first step toward becoming emotionally free of a past hurtful situation. This doesn't mean that you will always forget the hurt, but the event's emotional grip on you will no longer be as strong as it once was.

Each person is of ultimate worth to God, so we should be careful how we speak to people.

—Paul Andersen

Session NINE
Seeing Others Through "God-Glasses"

Discipleship Objective 9:

To identify yourself with Christ, you need to see and treat people the way Jesus did.

Loosening Up (15-20 minutes)

Public Put-Downs

Begin this session about put-downs by discussing the following questions:

• How do you generally react and feel when you are around someone who puts someone down or tells an offensive or derogatory joke?

• What would be an appropriate response to someone who says things to you that you don't appreciate hearing?

• When someone says something you consider offensive, what effect does this have on your attitude or disposition toward that person? Explain.

Faith-Building Follow-Up

Report on your experience with last session's Faith-Building Adventure.

Foundation (50-60 minutes)

An important but sometimes overlooked aspect of discipleship is Jesus' command to "love one another" (John 13:34). A part of this involves loving those we find difficult to like, loving those who have hurt us, and loving those who are different from us.

PREJUDGING

1. In what ways, obvious or subtle, do you think Christians tend to prejudge or not show the love of Christ?

If you have a large group, form smaller groups to answer the group discussion questions. Unless otherwise noted, answer the questions in your subgroup. At the end of the Foundation section, allow time for subgroups to report their answers to the whole group.

2. If comfortable doing so, tell about a time you were either prejudged or were guilty of prejudging.

3. Read 1 Samuel 16:1-7 and 1 Corinthians 1:26-29. On what basis would Samuel have made the choice of who was to be the next king if the choice had been his alone to make? Compare and contrast this to what God looks for.

FOLLOWING JESUS' STEPS

4. In John 4:1-42 we read about a cross-cultural encounter that Jesus had.

• What steps did Jesus take and how many barriers did Jesus cross in reaching out to the woman at the well?

Leader: For question 4, time permitting, read John 4:1-42. Or have a volunteer who completed the Personal Prep for Session Nine give a brief synopsis of Jesus' encounter with the Samaritan woman.

• What resulted from the risks Jesus was willing to take?

• What barriers tend to keep us from reaching out to others who are different than us?

• What practical points of application can we take from the example of Jesus' interaction with the Samaritan woman?

CALLED TO LOVE

5. Divide the following Scriptures between three or four subgroups. Have each group read its verses and discuss what they say about our responsibility to love. After a few minutes, each group should report their insights.

• Matthew 5:43-48	• Romans 13:8-10
• Luke 6:35-36	• Ephesians 5:1-2
• John 13:34-35	• 1 John 3:16
• John 15:12-14	• 1 John 4:7
• Romans 12:9-10	• 1 John 4:19-21

6. In Matthew 5:44-48 and Luke 6:35-36 Jesus commands us to love our enemies. As Christians, by what means are we able to do this? Explain.

7. Read Romans 12:14-21. According to these verses, what should be the standard of our conduct toward our enemies?

8. Read Matthew 6:14-15 and Mark 11:25. What role does forgiveness play in being able to love others?

9. Read John 17:20-26. What is Jesus' prayer for all Christians? Spend a couple of minutes in silent prayer. Is there anyone you are holding something against? Ask God to help you be able to forgive.

Taking It to Heart (15-20 minutes)

KEY VERSES

Form groups of two or three and review the Key Verses for this session:

- 1 Samuel 16:7

- 1 John 4:20-21

TALKING TO GOD

Before closing in prayer, share prayer requests. Be sure to include any updates to requests that were shared in the previous session.

Prayer Requests:

Looking Ahead: The discipleship focus in Session Ten—the last session of this course—is on reviewing the discipleship principles you have learned as well as considering the next steps in your discipleship experience. Once again, complete the Taking It to the House components. You'll be glad you did!

Taking It to the House

FAITH-BUILDING ADVENTURE

Your application challenge this week:

1. Ask yourself if there are changes you need to make to help you not prejudge people and to love people you don't like.

2. Record the changes you identified and commit to taking action on these points. Write down what you have decided to do.

3. If you have a friend from a different culture or race, ask your friend to share with you some of his or her experiences with being pre-judged. Ask questions (How did your friend feel? How did your friend respond and why?) and take notes.

4. Share with your friend any insights or observations you have made from this session.

Bonus challenge: If you did not complete the Personal Prep for Session Nine prior to this session, consider working through the "Moving Toward Love Through Forgiveness" exercise on page 138—especially if God has revealed to you people in your life that you need to forgive.

PERSONAL PREP FOR SESSION TEN

DAY 1

Key Verses for Session Ten

With Session Ten being the last session of this course, instead of receiving new verses, spend time reviewing all the Key Verses you've had.

- 1 Samuel 16:7
- Mark 1:35
- Luke 6:46
- Luke 9:23-25
- John 5:24
- John 15:7
- Romans 6:23
- Romans 10:9-10
- Galatians 2:20

- Ephesians 5:17-18
- Philippians 3:10
- Philippians 4:6-7
- 2 Timothy 3:16-17
- Hebrews 4:12
- 1 Peter 5:8-9
- 1 John 4:4
- 1 John 4:20-21

Session One: Getting Acquainted

• Look back over Session One. What is the main thing you learned?

_____

_____

• How did this session challenge you in your walk with God?

_____

_____

• What practice have you implemented or do you most want to apply in your life from this session?

_____

_____

DAY 2

Session Two: The Measure of a Christian

• Look back over Session Two. What is the main thing you learned?

_____

_____

• How did this session challenge you in your walk with God?

_____

_____

• What practice have you implemented or do you most want to apply in your life from this session?

_____

_____

Session Three: Following Christ

• Look back over Session Three. What is the main thing you learned?

_____

_____

• How did this session challenge you in your walk with God?

_____

_____

• What practice have you implemented or do you most want to apply in your life from this session?

_____

_____

DAY 3

Session Four: Developing Intimacy With God

• Look back over Session Four. What is the main thing you learned?

_____

_____

• How did this session challenge you in your walk with God?

_____

_____

• What practice have you implemented or do you most want to apply in your life from this session?

_____

_____

Session Five: Prayer — Talking and Listening to God

• Look back over Session Five. What is the main thing you learned?

_____

_____

• How did this session challenge you in your walk with God?

_____

_____

• What practice have you implemented or do you most want to apply in your life from this session?

_____

_____

DAY 4

Session Six: Bible Study — Digging Deeper

• Look back over Session Six. What is the main thing you learned?

_____

_____

• How did this session challenge you in your walk with God?

_____

_____

• What practice have you implemented or do you most want to apply in your life from this session?

_____

_____

Session Seven: The Holy Spirit and You

• Look back over Session Seven. What is the main thing you learned?

_____

_____

• How did this session challenge you in your walk with God?

_____

_____

• What practice have you implemented or do you most want to apply in your life from this session?

_____

_____

DAY 5

Session Eight: Knowing Your Enemy

• Look back over Session Eight. What is the main thing you learned?

_____

_____

• How did this session challenge you in your walk with God?

_____

_____

• What practice have you implemented or do you most want to apply in your life from this session?

_____

_____

Session Nine: Seeing Others Through "God-Glasses"

• Look back over Session Nine. What is the main thing you learned?

_____

_____

• How did this session challenge you in your walk with God?

_____

_____

• What practice have you implemented or do you most want to apply in your life from this session?

_____

_____

Session TEN

Next Steps

The focus of this session is to reflect on your experience with this course and to be challenged to the life of a disciple maker.

Loosening Up (15-20 minutes)

LOOKING BACK, LOOKING AHEAD

Congratulations! You have made it to the last session of this study. Reflect on your experience and what you would like to see happen next. Take a few minutes to think about the following questions and record your responses. Then discuss your responses.

• What expectations did you have coming into this group? How did your experience compare?

• What has been the highlight of this group for you?

• In considering this course as a whole, what has been the most important point or lesson for you?

FAITH-BUILDING FOLLOW-UP

Report on your experience with last session's Faith-Building Adventure.

• What would you like to see happen next for you or for this group?

Foundation (50-60 minutes)

Disciple makers will tell you that you will never take someone further than where you are spiritually. The truth of the previous statement reveals the necessity of us growing in our walk with God so that in turn we can help others grow.

REVIEW

Try and answer the following questions without referring back to the previous sessions.

> If you have a large group, form smaller groups to answer the group discussion questions. Unless otherwise noted, answer the questions in your subgroup. At the end of the Foundation section, allow time for subgroups to report their answers to the whole group.

1. What are the key elements of a personal faith story?

2. According to the Bible, what does it mean to be a Christian? What are some characteristics of a person who has become a Christian? Back up your answers with Scripture.

3. In your own words, what does it mean to serve Jesus as Lord of your life?

4. What has changed in the time you personally spend with God from before this course to now?

5. What new or renewed lesson about prayer have you learned?

6. In what way has the Bible impacted your life over the last few weeks?

7. What are ways the Holy Spirit ministers in the life of a Christian? Which of these ministries do you appreciate the most or need the most in your life right now?

8. What are some ways Christians can resist Satan?

9. How does God want us to view others? Explain.

These questions are one way to review some of what you have studied over the last several weeks. You have been exposed to a lot, yet you may feel there is still much that you don't know. It is a good sign if you feel this way. The best way to learn something is by teaching it. The same is true about discipleship. You now have more head knowledge about discipleship, but the heart knowledge will be gained through the experience of investing your life in the life of another.

YOU'VE ONLY JUST BEGUN!

10. Read Matthew 28:19-20. According to this passage, what are followers of Jesus called to? Is this call optional for you as a Christian? Explain.

11. Read John 15:8 and 2 Timothy 2:2. What are we told to do with spiritual truth we have learned? Practically, what are ways this can be done?

I trust that your participation in this group and course has been a challenging and exciting experience for you. My prayer is that you will now take the next step and ask God to send you someone you can make a spiritual investment in. Don't worry about being perfect; only God is perfect. You will learn more as you begin to disciple people than you learned by going through this study. The key is to be available, consistent, and patient. And if you think God is leading you to take a group through this study, pray about it; ask your leader for some tips; and don't be afraid to step out in faith and do it!

Taking It to Heart (15-20 minutes)

TALKING TO GOD

Before closing in prayer, share prayer requests. Be sure to include any updates to requests that were shared in the previous session.

Prayer Requests:

Taking It to the House

FAITH-BUILDING ADVENTURE

Pray. Ask God to send you someone to disciple. You may want to tell your pastor or other church staff that you have completed a discipleship course and are interested in opportunities to help others grow in their faith.

Group Publishing, Inc.
Attention: Product Development
P.O. Box 481
Loveland, CO 80539
Fax: (970) 679-4370

Evaluation for
Experiencing Discipleship

Please help Group Publishing, Inc., continue to provide innovative and useful resources for ministry. Please take a moment to fill out this evaluation and mail or fax it to us. Thanks!

● ● ●

1. As a whole, this book has been (circle one)

not very helpful   very helpful

1   2   3   4   5   6   7   8   9   10

2. The best things about this book:

3. Ways this book could be improved:

4. Things I will change because of this book:

5. Other books I'd like to see Group publish in the future:

6. Would you be interested in field-testing future Group products and giving us your feedback? If so, please fill in the information below:

Name _____

Church Name _____

Denomination _____ Church Size _____

Church Address _____

City _____ State _____ ZIP _____

Church Phone _____

E-mail _____